Dear Elep
Letters to Anim

Copyright © 2022 Florina Falce and Jane Bristowe

ISBN 978-1-945028-41-0

Published by The Art of Everyone

Please visit dearelephantbook.com
janebristowe.com
and theartofeveryone.com

CC BY-NC-SA: This license allows reusers to distribute, remix, adapt, and build upon the material in any medium or format for noncommercial purposes only, and only so long as attribution is given to the creator. If you remix, adapt, or build upon the material, you must license the modified material under identical terms.

Dear Elephant

Letters to Animals

Florina Falce

Jane Bristowe

The Art of Everyone
London, New York

"An understanding of the natural world and what's in it is a source of not only a great curiosity but great fulfilment. Young people — they care. They know that this is the world that they're going to grow up in, that they're going to spend the rest of their lives in. But, I think it's more idealistic than that. They actually believe that humanity, the human species, has no right to destroy and despoil, regardless."

—Sir David Attenborough

Letters

Dear Reader

Dear Elephant

Dear Meerkat Matriarch

Dear Flamingo

Dear Koala

Dear Ladybug

Dear Blue Whale

Dear Rhino

Dear Giraffe

Dear Frog

Dear Kingfisher

Dear Lobster

The Maintenance Crew

Acknowledgments

I love you x

Dear Reader

You are loved, too, but this book is about our love for our planet and what remains of the wild animal world. Did you know that more than ninety percent of the world's large animals (in other words, those weighing more than a few kilograms) are either humans or our domesticated animals? In the past 50 years alone, the wildlife population has halved. In his sensational 2017 book, *Homo Deus: A Brief History of Tomorrow*, Yuval Noah Harari draws attention to a few revealing comparisons, such as the world's wolf population of about 200,000, compared to the number of domesticated dogs, at 400 million. There are only 900,000 African buffalo versus 1.5 billion milk and beef cattle. It is well known that Homo sapiens have changed the global ecology—and equally known what the impact has been.

This book doesn't attempt to talk about what is already covered in detail by many environmentalists and advocacy groups that deal with biodiversity and climate change issues. Instead, we simply want to take the time to send some love notes to the wild during these challenging times, recognizing that the same Homo sapiens have always been inspired by the wild from the beginning of times to create stories, music, art and to wish for harmony with nature. Just the other day, I saw a video of a mama bear with her three cubs trying to cross a busy road. The cubs were anything but docile. They wanted to stay behind, climb a tree, play in the middle of the road. Cars were at standstill. Mama bear calmly and devotedly tried to pick up her cubs, not once yelling at them, not once threatening to cut out the honey or leave them behind. They managed to cross the road after a few trips back and forth. They also managed to go viral on social media, inspire and melt some (human) hearts.

We invite you, Dear Reader, to join our love message to the wild, and to feel connected with all life on this planet through love.

Florina and Jane
X

P.S. Our collaboration started in 2020 with the essay "The Maintenance Crew," which was published at *The Art of Everyone*. Jane's linocut art, borne out of her love for animals, inspired Florina to explore and write about her own feelings for the animals Jane had depicted. A copy of the essay is included in the last chapter.

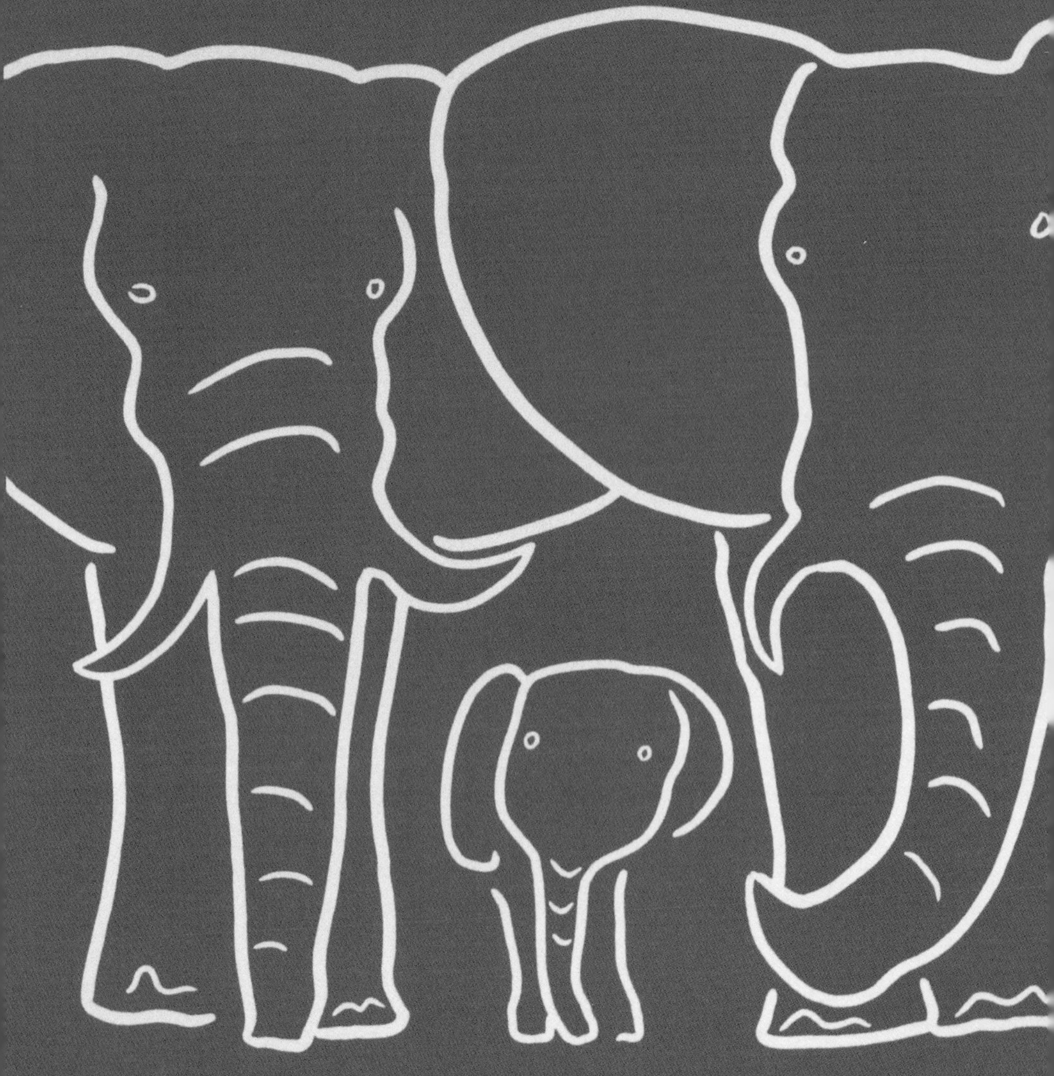

To: My Dear Elephant

From: Jane, Florina,
and Friends of Elephants

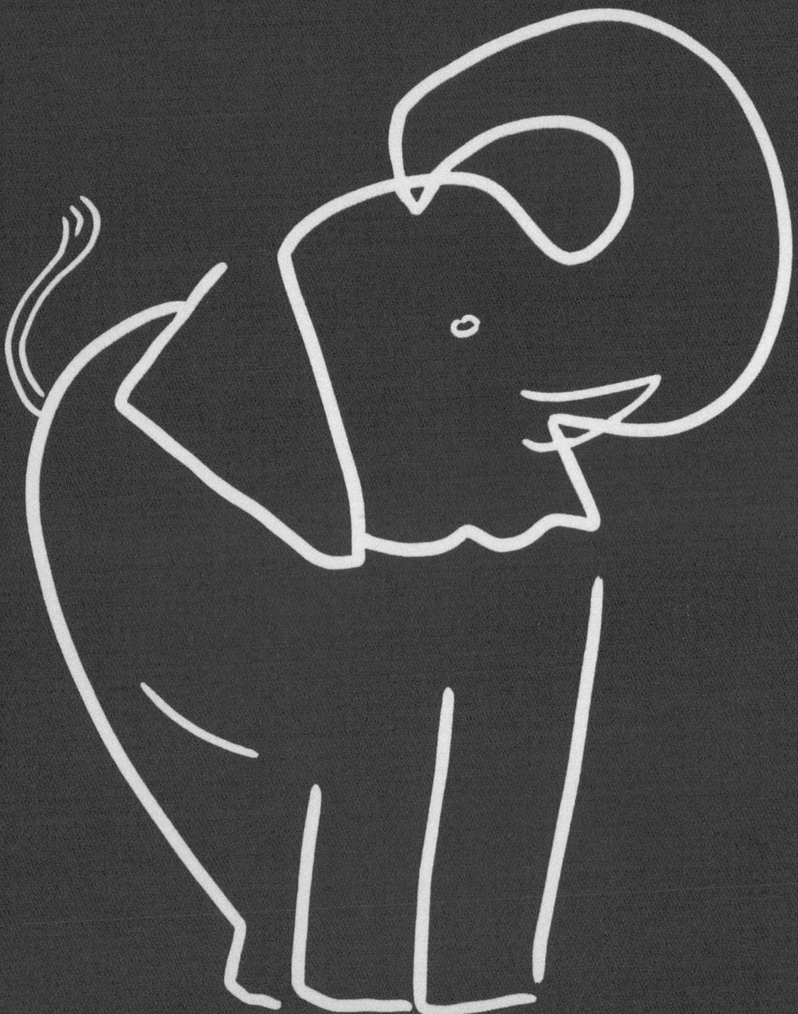

Dear Elephant,

Everything about you is monumental
Nature has sculpted mountains in your image
Montgó Massif in Spain, Xiangshan in Taiwan,
Elephant Rock in Iceland

Everything about you is ten thousand times
Bigger than a mouse
You really aren't afraid of rodents
The "mouse-in-the-trunk" is just a myth dating back centuries
To the ancient Greeks
Maybe the myth is not really about you
But about humans' own startled reaction to mice
Those little creatures can drive anyone crazy when scurrying across our private spaces

Your freedom is measured in thousands of square miles

Your big floppy ears make us imagine your flight

Your eyes are always moist with elephant tears (though you don't have tear ducts) —

Something to do with your semi-aquatic ancestry, not your feelings

You are a joyful sort.

A family guy.

At dusk, your stealthy presence in the forest echoes your humility

You retire in greatness when other animals go after their prey —

You eat plants and fruits

And how delicate the gesture

Picking up fruit with your long trunk!

No wonder you are a natural painter

Known to create valuable abstract art pieces when given the opportunity

The same trunk powerful enough to kill a lion with a single sweep!

I don't suppose that happens often —

Lions know better than to come close to you.

I know I won't come close
Even though your reputation is that
Of a gentle
Ten-ton
Giant.

I love you
x

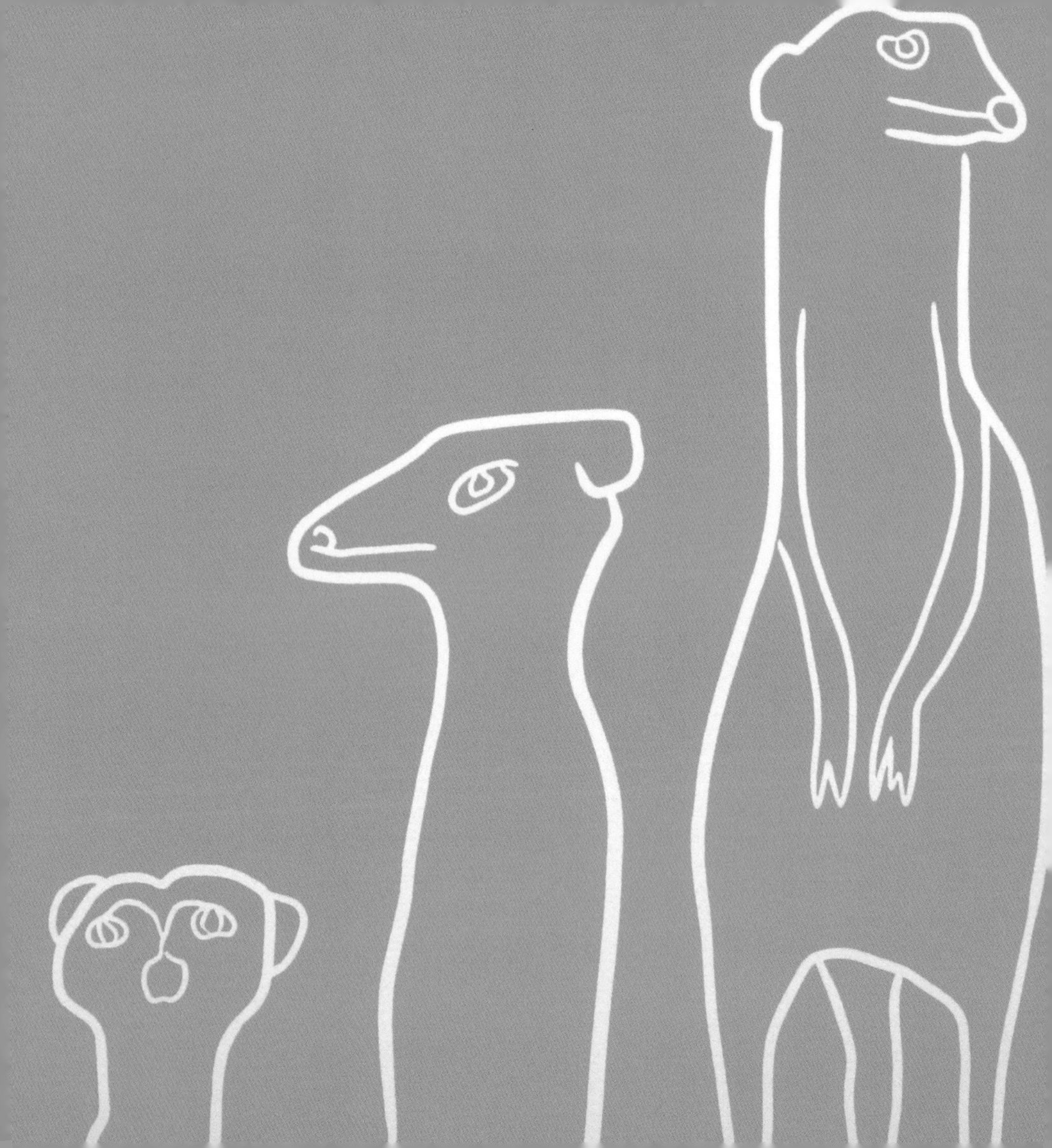

TO: My Dear Meerkat Matriarch

FROM: Jane, Florina,
and Friends of Meerkats

Dear Meerkat Matriarch,

I hear you are the boss, top banana, leader of the pack. You are not a "mere cat" (and not feline at all—rather a member of the mongoose family). Seriously, I think highly of you and of the role you play as the matriarch of your clan.

Did you know that our human ancestors were said to have lived in a matriarchal society some two million years ago. Who knows, it may be a myth, a fantasy, or maybe hope? I hope that humans can imagine, trust and encourage a world that values those qualities that are commonly considered "feminine," such as care, intuition, connection, vulnerability and devotion. I read there is an ancient tribal community that still exists in China, called "The Mosuo," where the female is at the centre of the society. It makes me happy.

When I say I think highly of you, my dear Meerkat Matriarch, it's for several reasons: you are the breadwinner, so to speak. Insects, rodents, lizards, you provide for your pups. That's not all; you also take care of your clan's organisation, burrows, friends. Your organisation includes a well-established sentry service by members of your clan to spot predators (birds of prey, snakes) and funnel everyone into hiding.

It's a lot, so you accept all the help you can get. While you go out, some of your tribe members stay behind to care for your pups. You'd kick them out of the gang if they didn't, am I right?

But that doesn't happen often because everyone knows what's in it for them: safety, companionship, survival. Everybody chips in and gives a hand (or a paw). In our society, many women try to do it all singlehandedly. They take care of kids, work, family life. Fulfilling, yes, but sometimes it's too much. There's something to be said for a clan life centred around support and community. Hats off to you! You may just be a role model.

I love you
x

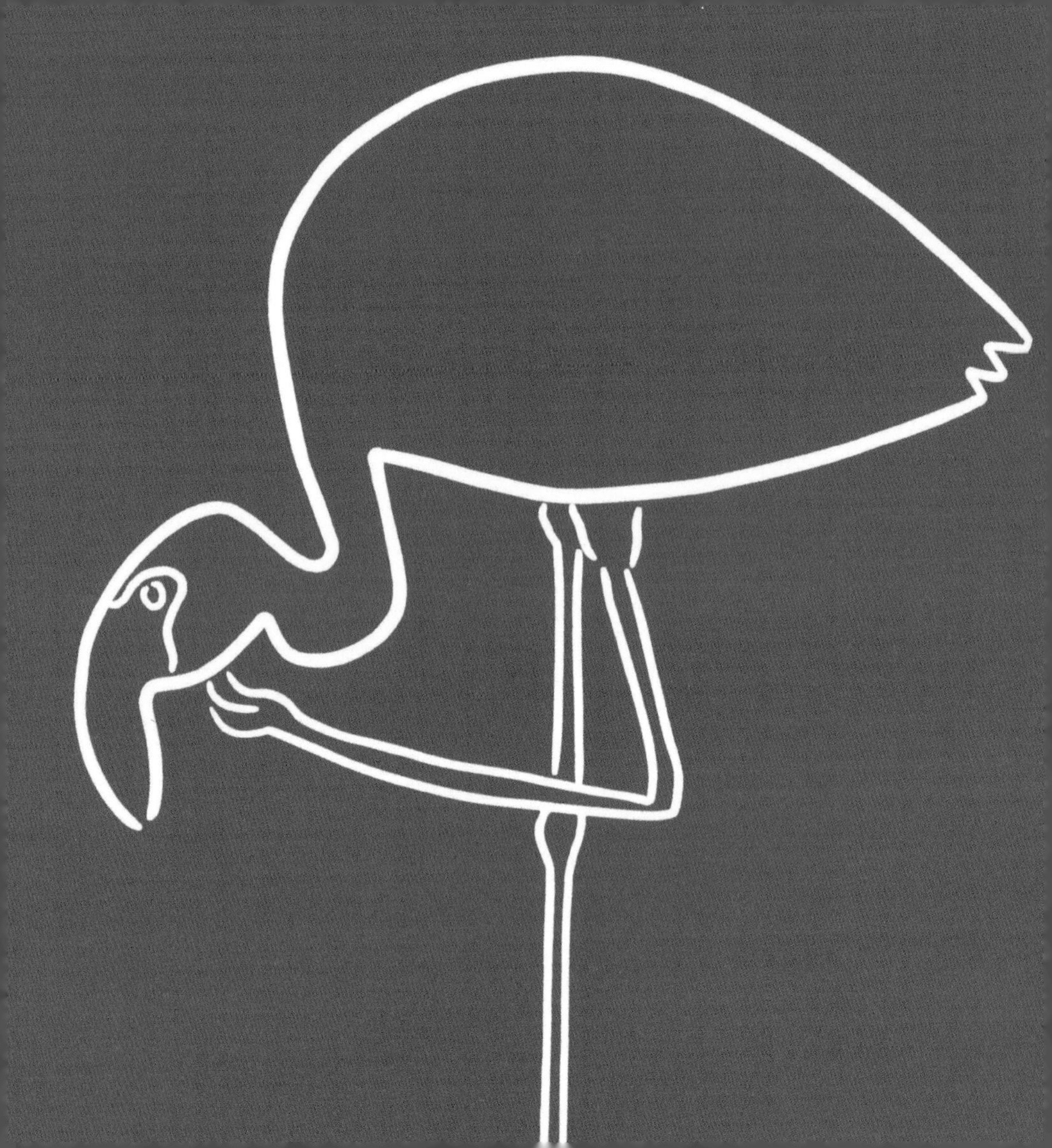

To: My Dear Flamingo

From: Jane, Florina,
and Friends of Flamingos

Dear Flamingo,

I love your pink attire! And when your good looks pop up somewhere new, I smile. I find you on cocktail glasses, beach bags, sandals and summer dresses. It makes me think of a highly desired (and much-needed) Caribbean vacation. By the way, I did not know that you are the national bird of the Bahamas, but that suits you well.

Cool name, too. Yours sounds like "flamenco" and for good reason. Vibrant and ecstatic, like Spanish dancers in their colourful dresses. About that, I was wondering why you picked pink for your feathers, and then I realized this all boils down to your shrimp-rich diet, which turned your birth costume of grey feathers to bright pink. I guess I am stuck with my natural hair colour. Three years of shrimp-eating (not to mention algae) is too high a price to pay.

Note to self: Consider a Halloween costume in the flamingo's image this fall. With high heels as well, to reach the bird's supermodel height of 6 feet. Here's an idea! Better yet, I may try and convince my friends to also dress up and we can turn into a flock of flamingos for one night of flamboyance.

Flamenco, flamboyance, flamingo, funny how our language evolved. It makes me wonder how you communicate. I assumed you were the chatty type, but I learned you rely on body language a lot — wing salutes, marching with your head high (really high), your neck stretching as mating rituals — and all this in front of your entire regiment, in person only, no virtual streaming except the water's reflection of your beauty. So, cheers to your splendour!

It's winter here in England as I write, and summer seems so far away, but I'm grateful you coloured my day with your flamboyant aura.

I love you
x

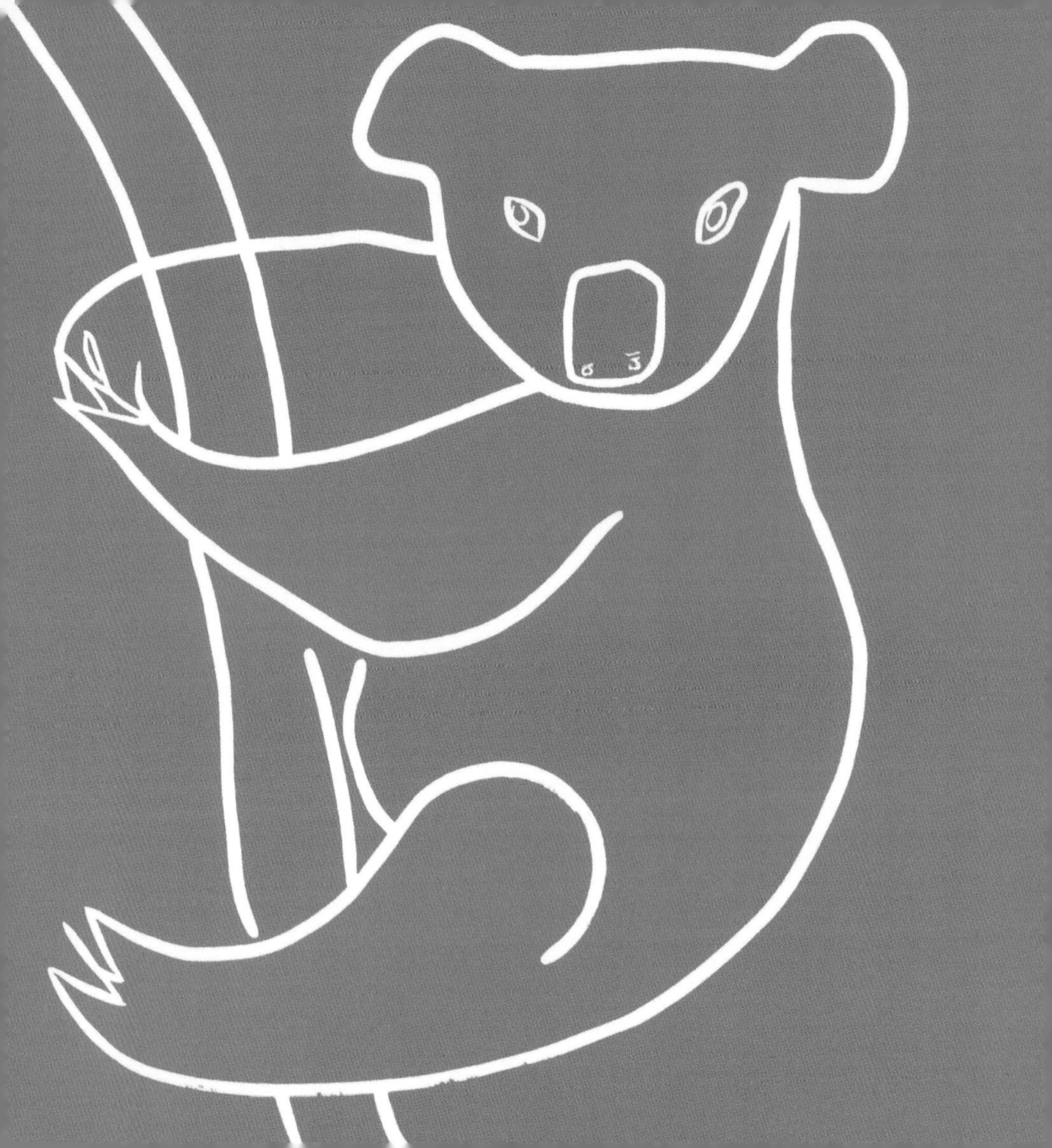

Dear Koala,

I just want to check in and see how you are doing. I know the last couple of years have been hard for you, with large fires engulfing your Australian habitat, which is supposed to be full of the tasty eucalyptus trees you like so much. I've seen you threatened, injured, scared and — some of you, fortunately — cared for.

Please know that I'm thinking of you and I cannot imagine a world without compassionate, curious looks! While you have been heavily hunted for your fur in the early 20th century, we seem to have found a way around the hunting now. We make plush toys in your image to cuddle with instead. You look like a teddy bear, even though you're not a bear but a marsupial. You are comforting and oh so lovable!

I still fear for you, but lots of us are watching out now. Grunt or bellow if you need a hand. I know you typically don't need much — eucalyptus leaves (a ton of them, or actually, just two pounds a day) and about eighteen hours of sleep daily up there in the trees. But I also fear for those trees. Stay safe, my cuddly friend!

I love you
x

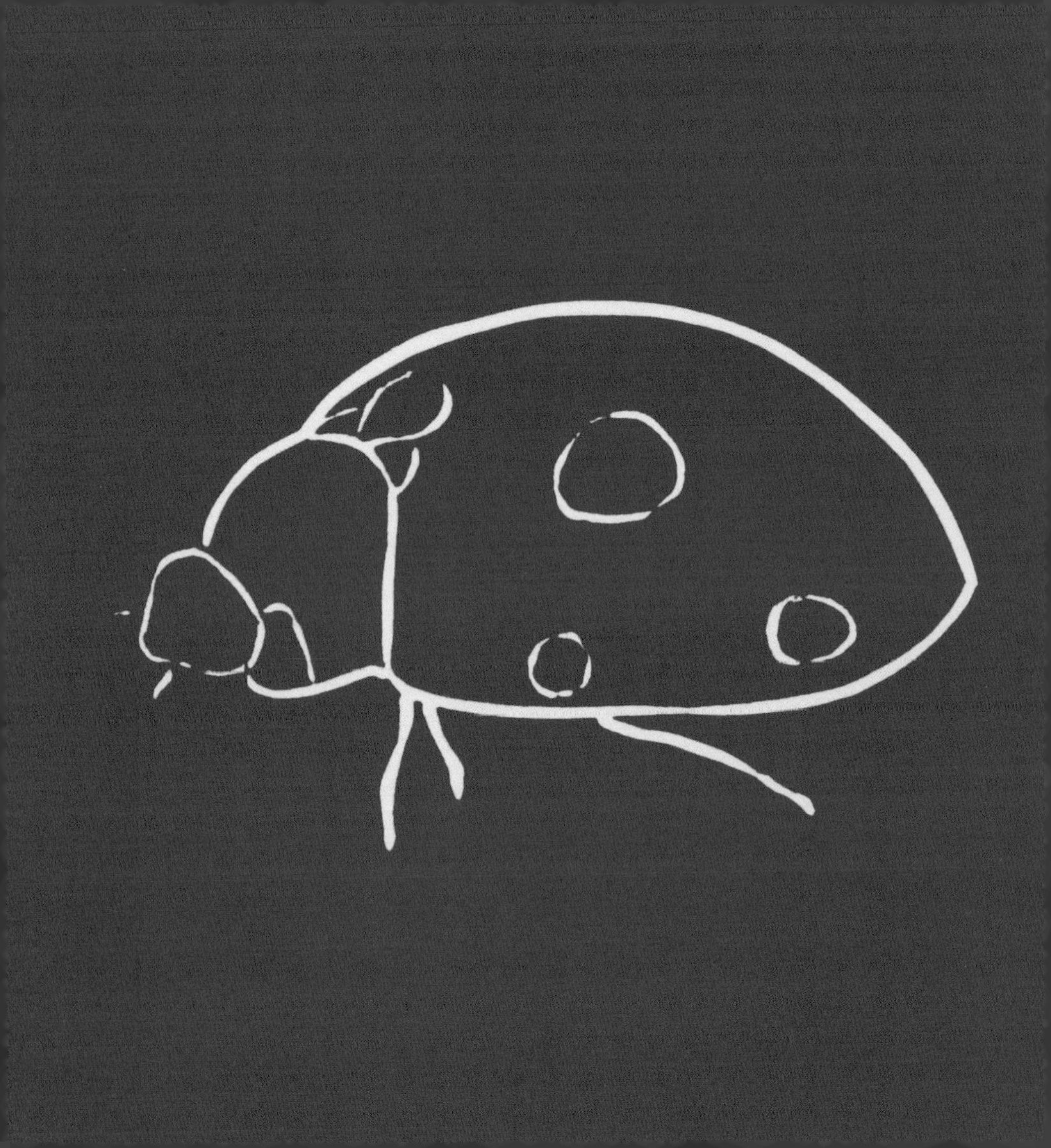

Dear Ladybug,

I'd like to ask you a favour. Would you allow our readers to draw a picture of you right here in this book? We aim to have as many of you as possible because we love you. You are so pretty and harmless, and we are grateful for your hard work protecting crops from other bugs.

Jane's drawing of you here is a perfect model, but our readers can follow their imagination. And they can't go wrong, since there are about 5,000 different species of you out there in the world, so every colour of the rainbow can be found. Even better, you are considered as a good luck charm in some cultures.

Here's another incentive to draw a couple! I remember a French nursery rhyme that went like this:

Coccinelle, demoiselle,	Ladybug, lady,
Bête à bon Dieu.	God's bug
Coccinelle, demoiselle,	Ladybug, lady,
Vole jusqu'aux cieux	Fly up to the sky
Petit point blanc, elle attend	Small white dot, she is waiting
Petit point rouge, elle bouge	Small red dot, she is moving
Petit point noir…	Small black dot …
Coccinelle, au revoir !	Ladybug, goodbye!

Silly rhymes if you ask me, but hey, at least you have a song dedicated to you. That's more than I can say. So here's to your Ladyship!

I love you
X

Share your drawing!
Use the hashtag:

#dearladybug

and see what others
drew, too!

Draw a Ladybug!

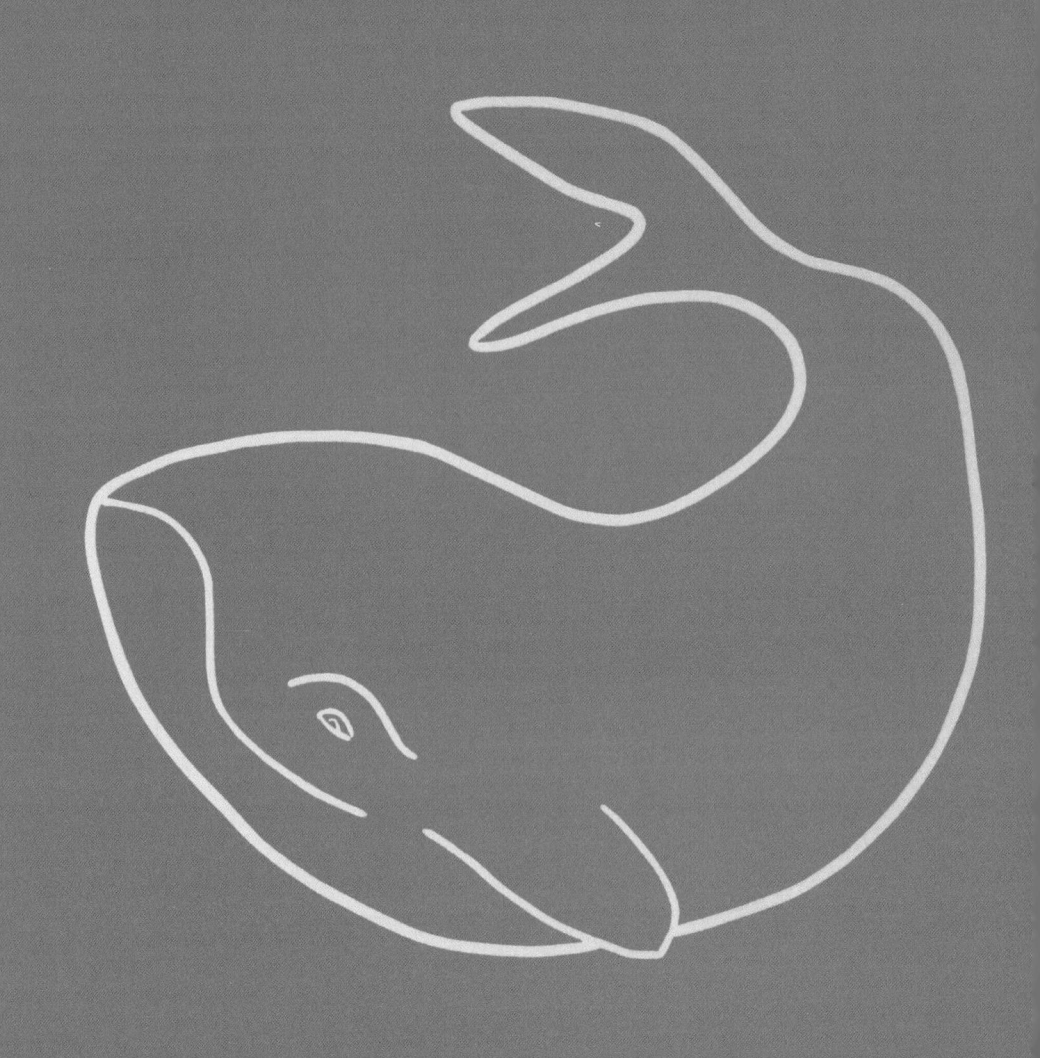

To: My Dear Blue Whale

From: Jane, Florina,
and Friends of Whales

Dear Blue Whale,

I've never seen you, but I once went on a humpback whale watching cruise out of the Boston harbour in Massachusetts, USA

I remember the October wind messing up my hair and forcing me to wear gloves

I remember the sky and the ocean had the same dark grey colour

But I don't remember where the water drops on my cheeks came from

I don't recall having had any reason to weep

I remember boarding a 50-footer and pausing — what if the whales mistake it for a toy?

I don't remember much about the whales themselves

Except that they were playing hide-and-seek and I loved their playfulness

What I remember most vividly was the captain yelling — 11 o'clock! 3 o'clock!

It was meant to direct our eyes us towards the whales, but I sometimes missed them, looking a moment too late.

Browsing through these memories makes me smile. I imagine how silly this might have looked seeing us rushing almost uncontrollably from port to starboard, camera at the ready. But I loved everyone's playfulness. Otherwise serious people, hungry to see something new.

I already knew that you, my dear Blue Whale, were the largest animal gracing the face of our planet. But I was in awe to learn that you can weigh up to 150 tons. That's big—that's 24 elephants. Or about 2,000 of us, gallivanting on our boats. No, I didn't see you in Boston, or any of your siblings. I saw humpback whales instead. Much smaller than you.

But I want to believe that you are just as playful as they were.

I'd love to play with you too but last I checked you were still classified as an endangered species. And you prefer roaming the Arctic. I don't have warm enough gloves for that, so I send you this letter instead. I hope you'll stick around. I'll do my best to help.

I love you
x

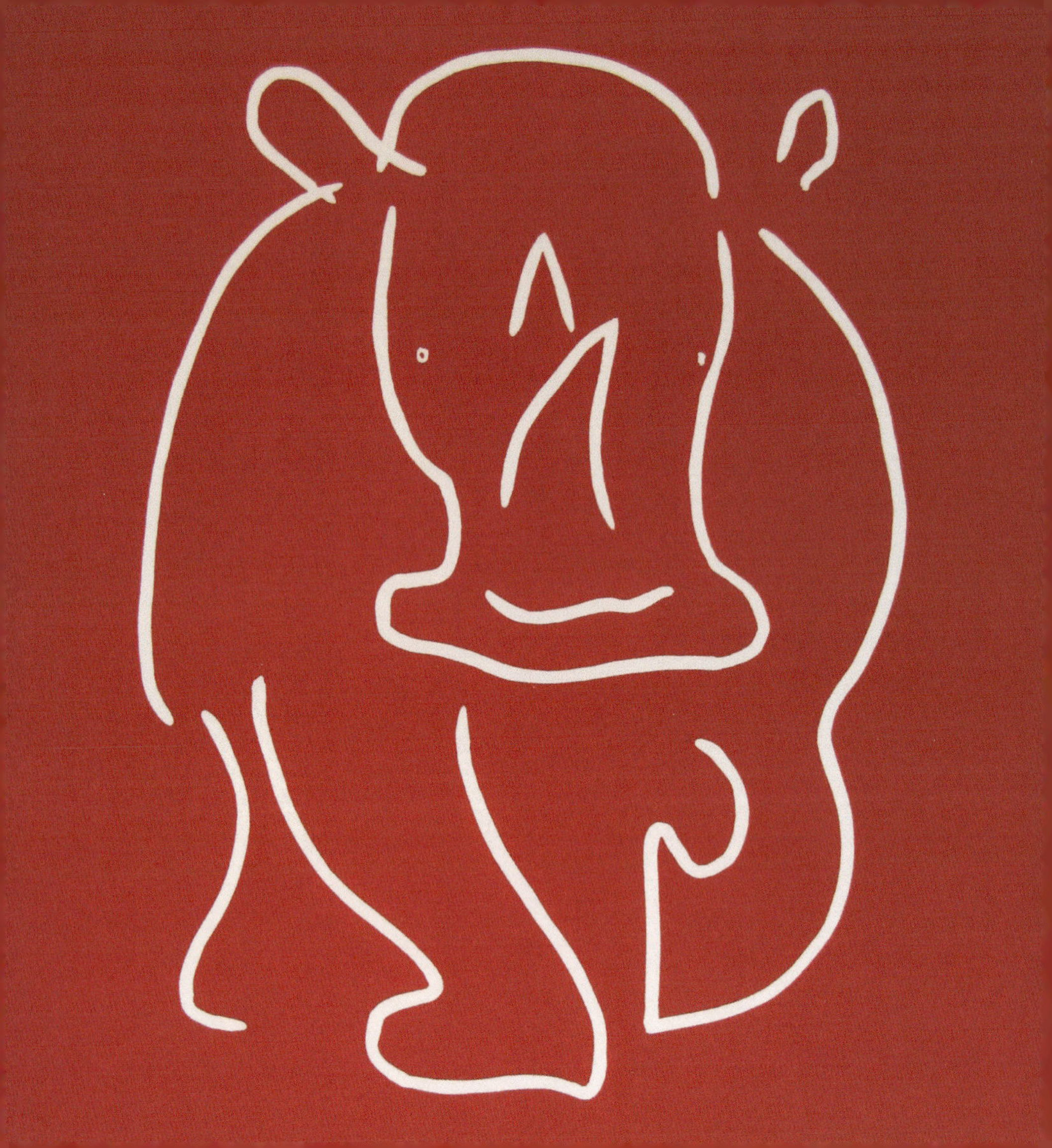

Dear Rhino,

I thought you'd like to know how humans understand your characteristics. We think of you as:

Intelligent

Agile

Inquisitive

Gentle

Kind

A unicorn

An actual animal that looked like you called the Siberian Unicorn was discovered to have lived 39,000 years ago. It may very well be your ancestor, and may have inspired the Unicorn myth based on its long single horn—who knows. I prefer to believe you carry the magic in your DNA.

Please stay safe! I heard about poachers coming after you, and about your habitat loss, but you are strong, and loved, and you matter to most of us. You know how I know? I talk to unicorns—they are just projections of your remarkable spirit.

I love you
X

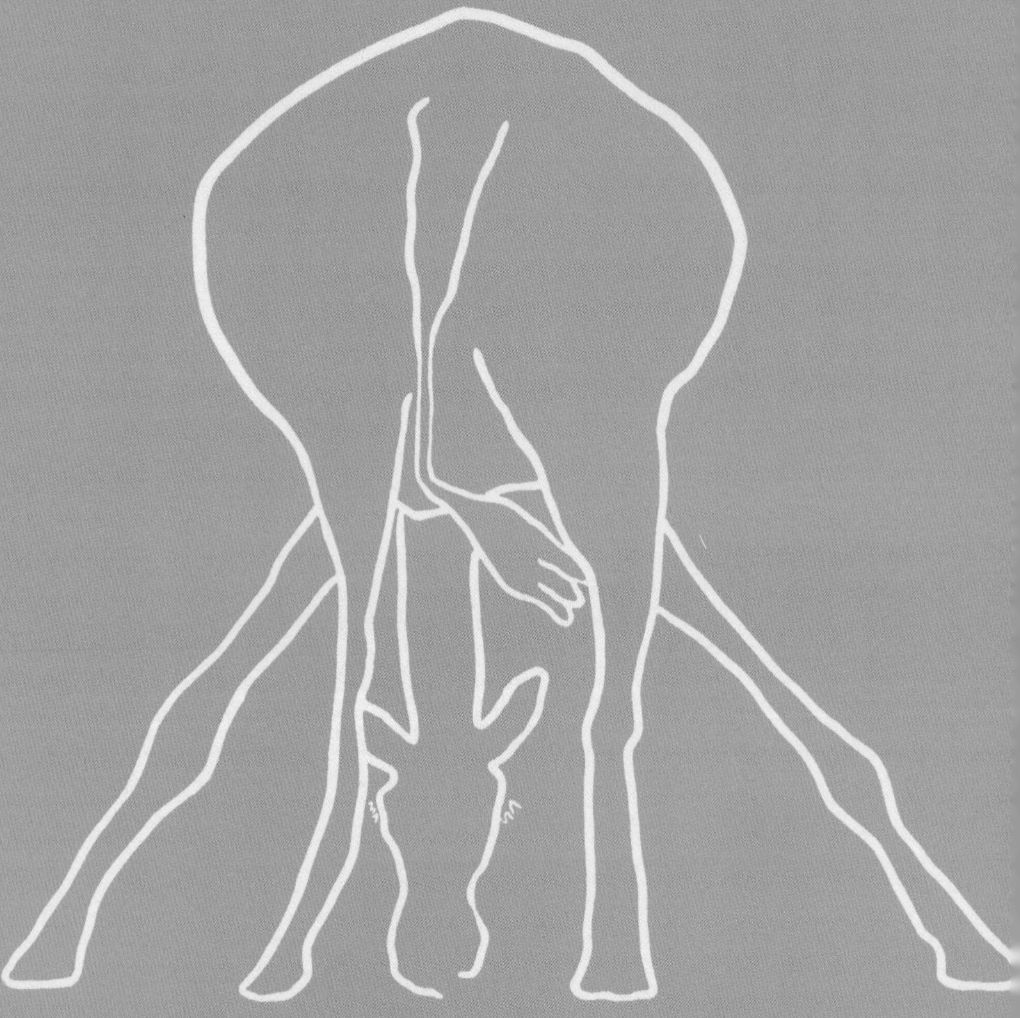

Dear Giraffe,

Here is a picture of you drinking water.

At first I thought you were practising a Downward Facing Dog yoga pose. You seem so flexible and graceful—as if you're curtsying.

I read that you are also very athletic, running as fast as 35 miles per hour—faster than I can achieve in my car as I tool around the London streets. And believe me, most of the time there is so much traffic I can barely reach your 10 mph cruising speed. I don't think you would face speed limit violation risks there in the African savannah, but I know you must deal with your own (real) challenges, like an encounter with a hungry lion, for example. I read that sadly, around 50% of young giraffes do not make it past the age of 6 months due to predation. Is it this constant threat from predators that keeps you awake at night? Just thirty minutes of sleep! How do you get through the day?

Next time I feel frustrated with traffic, or I have trouble sleeping, I'll remember I'm not in any real danger.

Be well my friend.

I love you
X

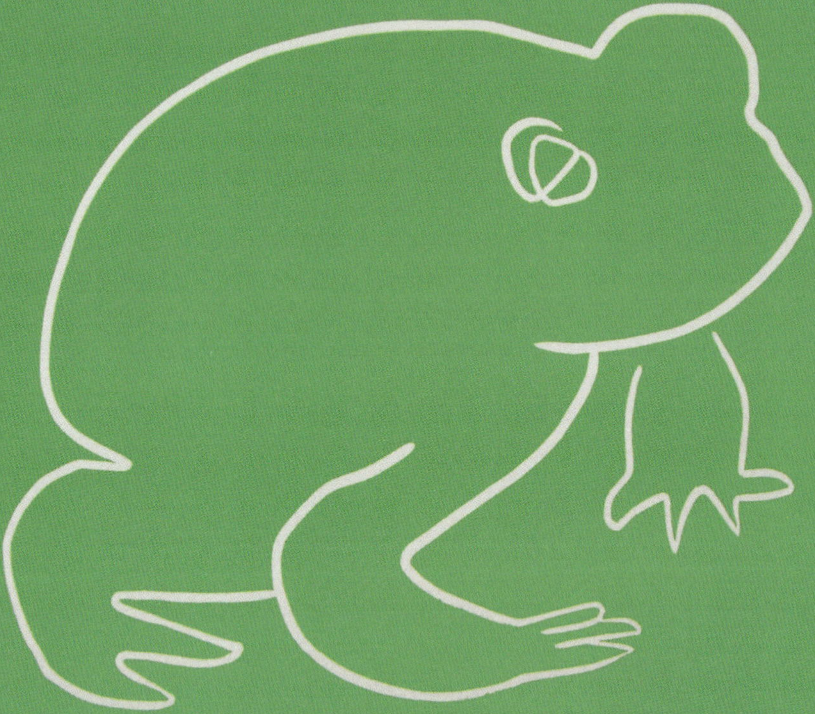

To: My Dear Frog

From: Jane, Florina,
and Friends of Frogs

Dear Frog,

Did you know you are a very popular character in children's books? From the well-known fairy tale published by the Brothers Grimm, *The Frog Prince*, to Beatrix Potter's *The Tale of Jeremy Fisher*, to *Frog and Toad* by Arnold Lobel and *City Dog, Country Frog* by Mo Willems. There are probably many more — *Fabulous Frogs* by Martin Jenkins.

What makes you so popular, I wonder?

I know you play an important role in our planet's ecosystem, even when you're just a tadpole keeping the waterways clean. With your darting tongue you keep bug populations in check. I even like to hear your loud croaks by the lake. Still, you are not seen as a beauty queen exactly, and your slimy nature does not make you very appealing to befriend, or hold, let alone kiss.

What I overlooked, however, was a more symbolic aspect of your nature. Your metamorphosis from tadpole to frog opens up the idea of transforming again into something even more wonderful.

The frog in the fairy tale who transforms into a charming prince bears immense significance, especially for kids who need role models of hope, possibility and magic to imagine and believe in their own potential for transformation.

I can see how that slimy skin of yours could be a symbol of your modesty and vulnerability—a temporary condition you accept with princely dignity.

Now, I may not necessarily want to kiss you, but from this slight distance, I salute your good works.

I love you
x

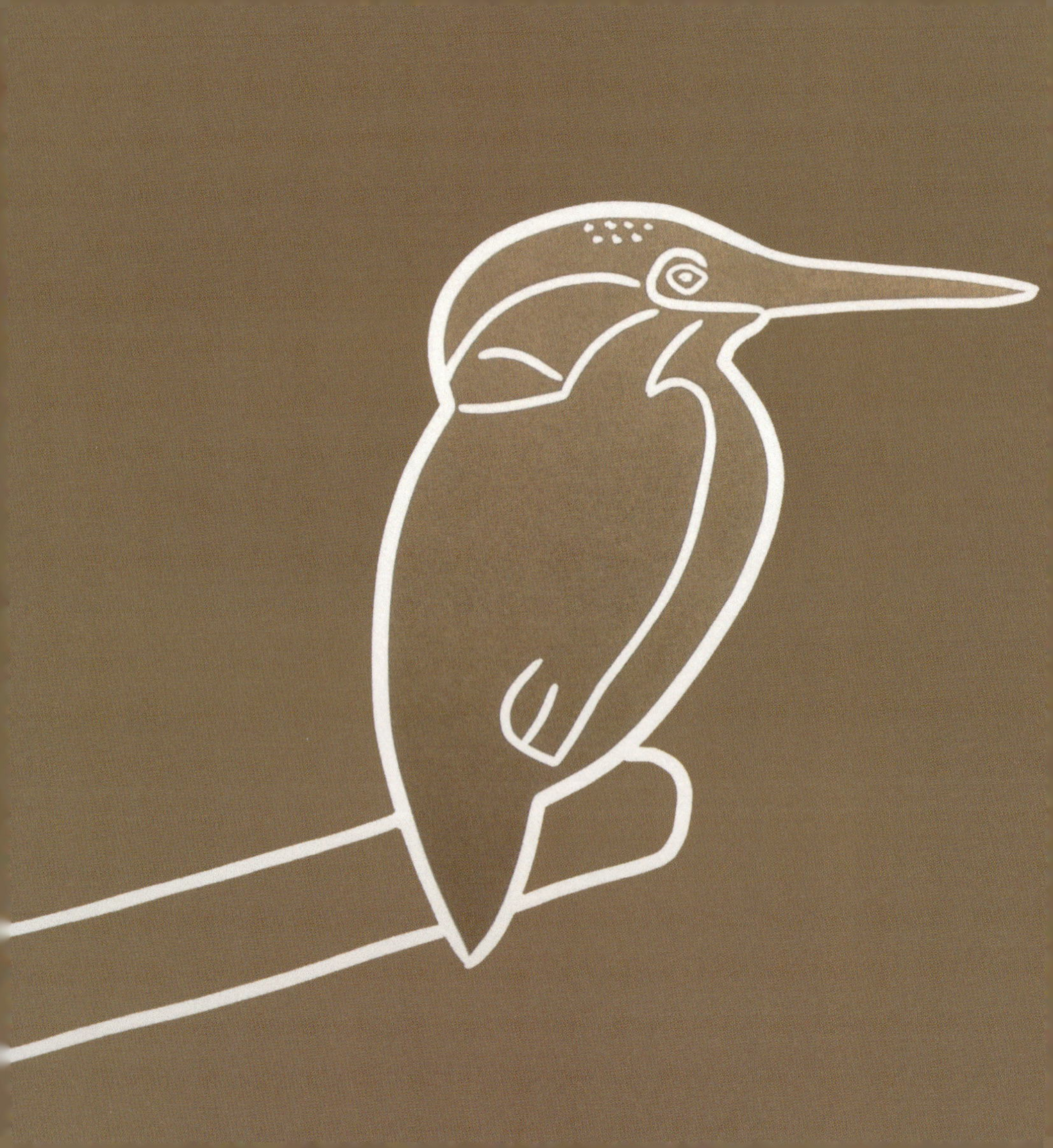

Dear Kingfisher,

What a fascinating bird you are!

Bird watchers are happy to spend hours in a bird hide (a camouflaged shelter) to see you perched on a pole, planning the next dive to catch a fish, shrimp, or tadpole. They know how rewarding it is to see the light showering your feathers with the most brilliant blue-green-turquoise-red-gold colours when you spread your wings to fly!

Equally rewarding, I imagine, is to see your stocky body and long, thick, dagger-shaped bill immersed in the water to catch the fish.

It is the form of your bill that cuts so cleanly into the water, with barely a splash, that prompted a young Japanese engineer named Makatsu (a passionate birdwatcher) to look at its shape as a solution for the design of the high-speed bullet trains. Those trains, while very fast, produced a troubling loud noise called "sonic boom" when passing through tunnels.

And so, after research and trials, the Japanese turned the nose of their bullet trains into a shape very similar to your beak.

Isn't that fascinating? I thought you'd like to know.

I love you
x

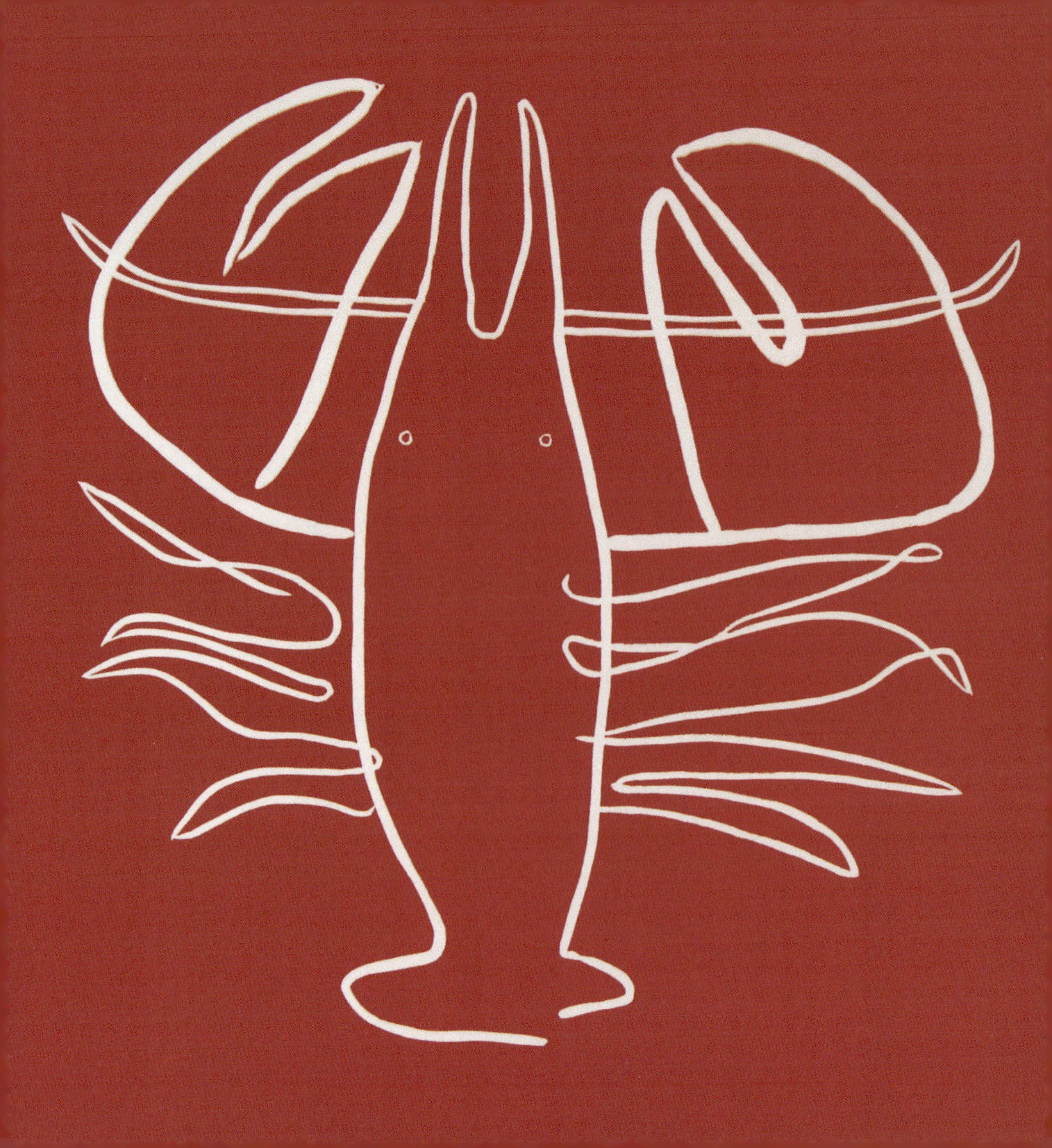

To: My Dear Lobster

From: Jane, Florina,
and Friends of Lobster

Dear Lobster,

I have a confession to make. It comes after I read an essay by David Foster Wallace called "Consider the Lobster," originally published in August 2004 by *Gourmet* magazine. By the title, one would expect to read an activist pamphlet trying to influence the readers' thinking on matters related to lobsters. But I read it like a documentary. At first.

There are so many things to learn. For example, you are viewed as a giant sea insect dating from the Jurassic period, both a hunter and scavenger. You are seen as the garbageman of the sea, and before you became a delicacy in the 19th century, you fed the lower classes mainly due to your abundance.

And then I read about cooking practices. I've never cooked a lobster, but have I sometimes enjoyed a lobster dish on a summer evening by the sea accompanied by a glass of rose wine (or maybe I preferred bubbles)? I have.

Have I imagined you were kidnapped from your home at the bottom of the sea, thrown alive in a kettle with boiling water from which you are desperately trying to escape by hooking your claws over the kettle's rim? I have not.

Have I thought of future generations considering present eating practices the same way we now view Nero's entertainment, or Aztec sacrifices? I may have heard my plant-eating, not-so-subtle teenager bring this up.

Faced with a lobster mac and cheese moral dilemma, would I have the will power to decline, or would I ask if it was ethically prepared (which apparently involves stabbing the lobster before boiling)? I don't know, my dear lobster. Do you believe "a fault (sin?) confessed is half redressed," as the old saying goes?

I love you
x

The Maintenance Crew

A Note on The Maintenance Crew

This story is about endangered animals. It involves three hand-picked characters—a snow leopard, a colony of bees, and a turtle—whose heroic qualities will inspire humans to join a global maintenance project these animals are leading for the benefit of our planet Earth and all its inhabitants.

Now, the stories.

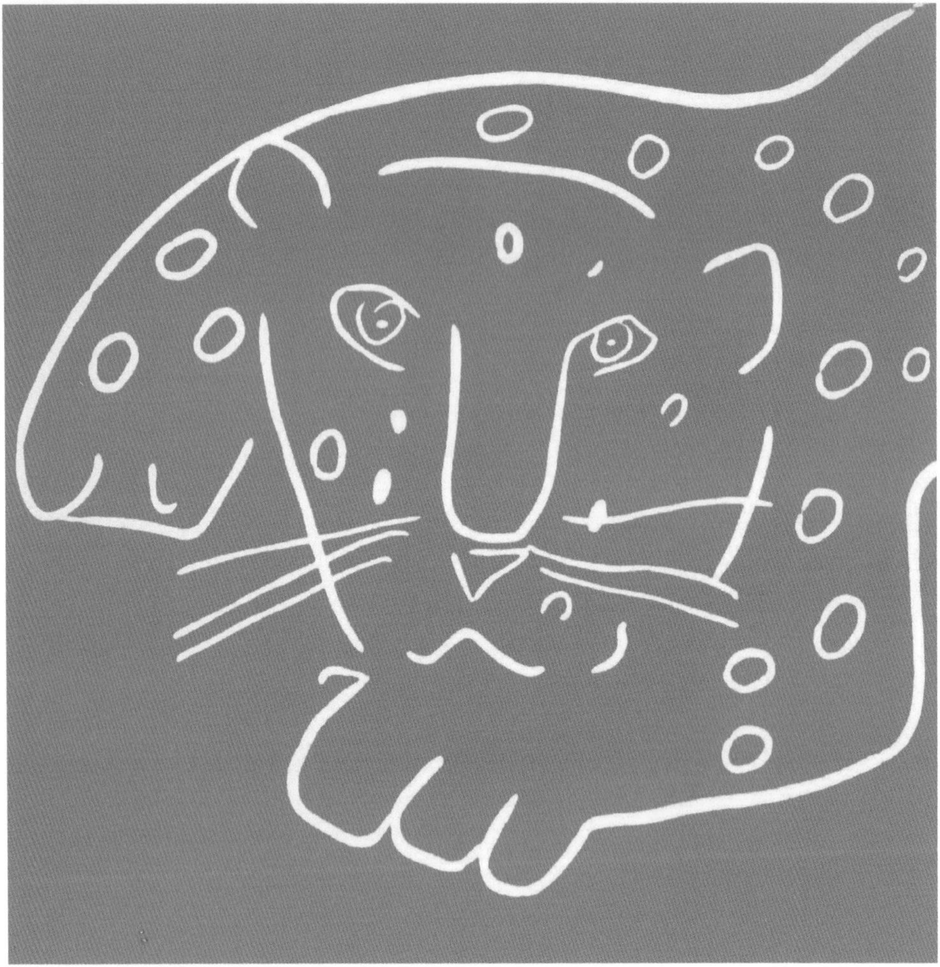

The Snow Leopard

Our family doesn't have a pet. We've been having cravings for a little dog for a while but we had to painfully decline our daughter's requests (too much maintenance!) for any kind of pet many times (what! not even a duck?).

Yet many times she got pretty close to breaking the resistance wall.

I remember it was the first month after moving to London when having a pet could have made a difference. One difference could have been that I would now write about our dog and not about white snow leopards, turtles or bees.

Although switching from domestic pets to the wild animal kingdom may feel like pet obsession in disguise, something else was unfolding.

Five years ago, we were walking in the charming streets of our newly adopted Fulham reality, dancing around the pet topic with carefully selected adult excuses, heavy with rationalisation. But Fulham is nothing like the Upper West Side of Manhattan, where we moved from. Fulham is a neighbourhood in London that seems to have been specially created to welcome families with pets, with its houses with outdoor spaces, parks with dog toilets, and streets patrolled by what feels like armies of eager-to-please Golden Retrievers, affectionate Pomeranians, the noblest of Spaniels, not to mention the popularity ladder climbers, the Pugs. This did not escape the longing eye of our very perceptive child.

So our excuses were out of context, unconvincing and empty.

And then a miracle happened. Right there across from our neighbourhood restaurant (pets welcome on the terrace!) were people selling snow leopards. Now, forget about a dog, who doesn't like snow leopards!? Who wouldn't want to grab one in their arms and cuddle and run away with it?

Despite some reservations regarding a few minor maintenance details for such an affair, there we were, aspiring snow leopard owners, impatiently queuing for a new adventure, my mind on a slippery slope, rushing to make the guest room as welcoming as possible, starting to google basic snow leopard necessities and care...when all of a sudden we were next.

The welcoming smile from the seller was just the confirmation we needed that we were doing the right thing.

He kindly started to run through a series of prepared lines which seemed to assess our adequacy as future snow leopard owners. Do we have a bank account, would we be willing to provide a direct deposit for the monthly payments, are we in our sane and responsible minds? We are.

Are we?

While my mind was ordering pet food, my husband and my daughter sealed the deal. They proudly held in their hands a full adoption package of what proved to be a year of long-distance relationship with a snow leopard. Regularly, my daughter would receive letters about the well-being of her snow leopard from the wild, where it was living a happy and protected life, carrying his soft, spotty, furry silhouette with elegance and dignity, somewhere in the Himalayas or the Siberian mountains and not here in the heart of Fulham and the comfort of my guest room.

Why did I feel a tingle of disappointment running through my spine all of a sudden? Did I envision a fairy tale adventure in which the next-door neighbour was none other than Princess Jasmine and her Rajah tiger, with whom I was starting to plan pet dates already?

Right. None of this saga proved to be part of the adoption papers. What I discovered, instead, were some chilling facts about these animals.

They come with a warning. R rated for violence and destruction.

It starts with wild Argali sheep, born in the food chain to feed the snow leopards. They thrive on being food for the higher-ups. No complaints. Gentlemen's agreement. Both parties have a mutual understanding of their role.

Then humans come in with no part in the treaty and no understanding and kill the sheep.

But humans have livestock. Why would we need the wild sheep, anyway?

The snow leopard is really hungry and angry, and the livestock looks almost like the Argali.

He has no choice.

Humans have a choice. But we kill the snow leopard. Retaliatory, point blank.

And then there is our soft killing. The one that melts the snow and kills from the bottom up. They call it climate change. I call it the silent weapon of mass destruction.

Let the peaks of the Himalayas be the judge.

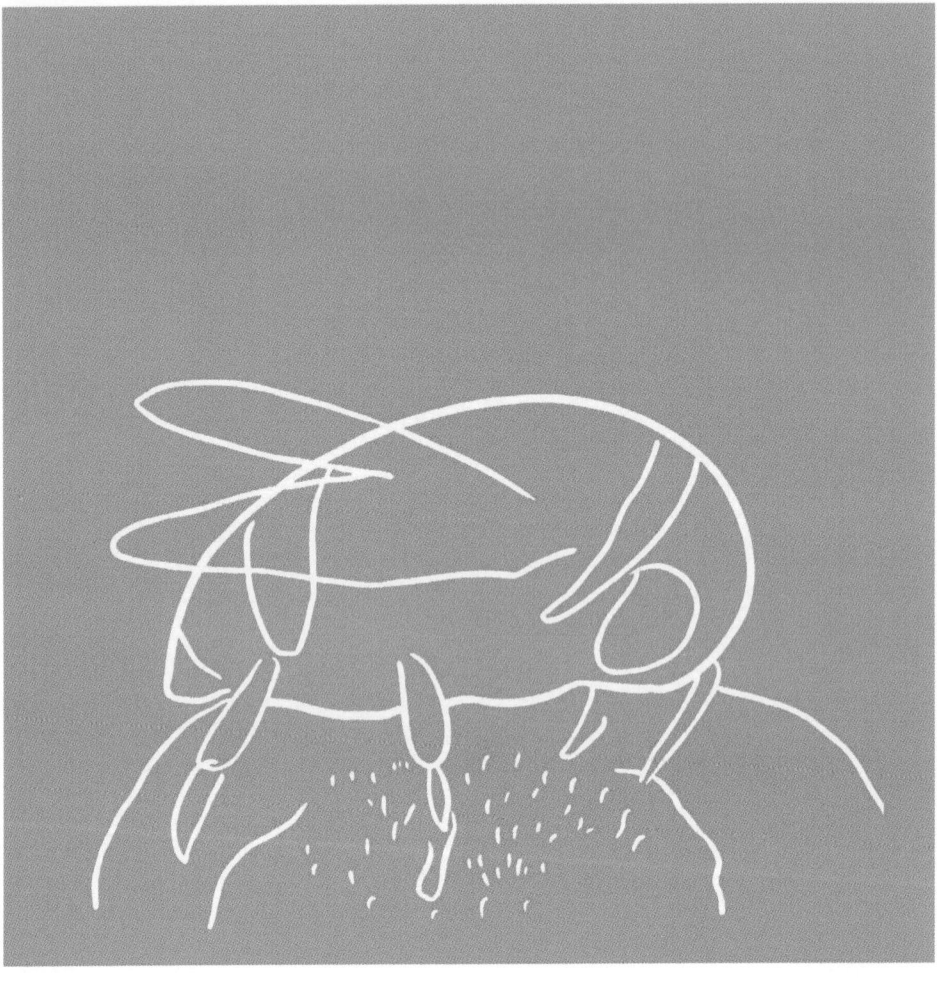

BEES

Bees and I have something in common: We love lavender.

I discovered how much I loved lavender backwards. I was once recommended essential lavender oil for good sleep. Then for a runny nose, back pain, mosquito bites, stress, to put in apricot and lavender cake, as a linen and vacuum cleaner freshener, as moth repellent, mood enhancement, to sooth kitchen burns and a few other things I'm sure I'll remember later.

This miracle oil certainly deserves its own story, but let's say for now that I did what anybody else would do. I wanted to learn more about it, so I planted a bush of lavender in my garden. I was right to do so.

It became my symbol of abundance, simplicity and serenity. Most importantly, it became the literal home to a colony of bees. It felt similar to looking for a pet dog and instead bringing home a snow leopard. Only this time, the bees were not in a land far, far away, but in my garden. We greet each other daily. They shared with me a few stinging facts, and I will share my fears.

A few stinging facts[1]:

- 30 to 40 percent of our food is available because of pollination by honeybees.
- One hive produces 50 to 100 pounds of honey in a year, depending on the health of the hive.
- Bumblebees vibrate at the musical note of C, the perfect frequency to open the tomato flower for pollination.
- Every worker bee goes through the same progression of jobs — housekeepers, undertakers, nurses of the young worker bees, attendants to the queen bee and, lastly, those who collect the nectar for the hive.
- Honey is the oldest medicine; it will never go bad if kept in a sealed container.
- Bees have a highly developed intestinal flora, like humans.

---

1   Source: theecologycenter.org

But they don't drink alcohol, take antibiotics or eat animal fats. They exercise all day. Their flora is thriving.

A few of my fears:

- Bees are threatened by climate change and human activities.
- Bees may become extinct and thus so will humans.
- Or, humans may invent artificial pollinators that have no eyes, no wings, no intestinal flora, no magnificence, no buzz.
- My lavender will die of loneliness.
- I will suffer insomnia.
- Or I will have nightmares where there is one jar of honey left in the world and it gets spoiled.
- Or I will go to Mars — unwillingly.

I fear predictable ends.

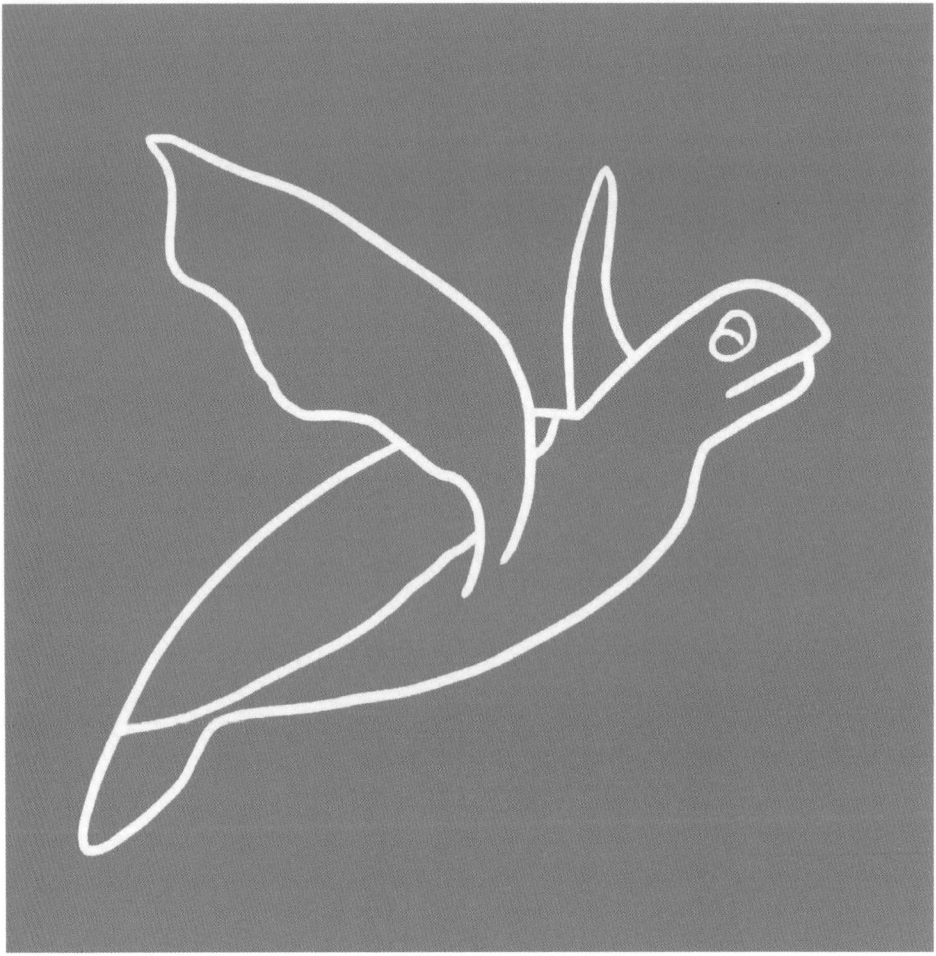

Turtles

There is a genesis to every story and this one starts with the Tortoise that figures in the La Fontaine fable — *The Hare and the Tortoise*.

My family keeps a collection of fables handy for inspiration. There is nothing like animal wisdom, and what I like the most in these fables is that it is often the smallest, the weakest, the slowest or the most unexpected animals that impersonate the sages and share life lessons in the most nonchalant and penetrating way.

Naturally, we became very attached to the Tortoise. She fits the profile of someone I would love to hang out with. She is slow but smart, witty, tenacious, courageous, bold. Bold is what I like the most. There is a form of acceptance and freedom in boldness. The Tortoise tried neither to grow longer legs, nor to get rid of her house to outrun the hare. She managed things in her way. Diplomatically, transparently and yes, perhaps a bit mischievously.

I want to be like her and challenge the world to a race against the development of silent weapons of mass destruction. While tortoises are exclusively land-dwelling, they are part of the larger turtles family that includes both land and sea creatures.

My friend Jane Bristowe found a beautiful way to acknowledge sea turtles. Her linocut art captures their boldness with such mastery and perception that I dived right into the turtles' world, deep down into the sea. Their reality is chilling. As chilling as that of the snow leopards.

Human activities such as poaching and over-exploitation, accidental entanglement in fishing gear, habitat destruction that has been going on for the past 200 years, together with climate change, have all led to dramatic reductions in their population. Nearly all species of sea turtles are now classified as endangered, with three of the seven existing species being critically endangered.

But ending the Turtle story on this note doesn't feel right.

I didn't have to leave it to chance this time, to coincidentally run into a sea turtle adoption crew in Fulham.

I looked for the crew myself, and I can't wait to see my child's eyes brighten when the adoption package arrives!

It is that light in her eyes every time we talk about animals that makes symbolic adoptions feel real.

Spotlight on The Maintenance Crew

There is nothing random about my choice of animals for this article. Although they are just three of the many species that are endangered to the point of almost no return, these creatures are among those animals in our planet's maintenance crew, whose work extends from the mountain tops to the meadows to the deep-sea waters.

The snow leopard, as a top predator in its habitat, plays an important ecological role in controlling prey populations and weeding out the sick, weak and injured. Predation keeps prey populations from destroying the vegetation.

They may not be the ideal in-home family pets (they are rather solitary and elusive cats), but they are guardians of their territory, with a sensible eye for checks and balances.

I imagine them climbing the highest peaks to get the pulse of their habitat, patrolling many miles of snowy terrain daily, inspecting, cleaning up, directing the sheep herds to maintain the pastures, and still being able to fit in some time for contemplation. The view from up there must be something…. Now, I would feel good about a day like this. Tired but good.

Bees also help to maintain life on Earth in a big way. There are billions of us benefiting one way or another from their hard work. They don't turn water into wine, but they do support healthy vineyards with diverse ecosystems, and they do turn flowers into food. And they are food themselves for skunks, hive beetles and others in the gentlemen's agreement.

Turtles are a fundamental link in marine ecosystems. These seagrass grazers, sponge eaters, jellyfish controllers help maintain the health of seagrass beds and coral reefs.

But their maintenance work doesn't stop at the bottom of the water; they also provide for some inhabitants of the land. Wildlife on the beaches—from small mammals to birds, to coastal vegetation—benefit by eating their eggs and hatchlings.

Plus, they are cute in an ancient kind of way. They go back 100 million years.

How many other species on Earth can claim this milestone?

And here come humans. They have consciousness, empathy, genius, they speak, they laugh, they read, they write, they see and taste beauty—wouldn't it be a shame if all these achievements were wasted by pushing the wrong limits, those of destruction?

Why not use our infinite capacities to create abundance and beauty and become part of the maintenance crew ourselves?

Indeed, conservation efforts have already started through organisations such as worldwildlife.org, bumblebeeconservation.org and many other local, national and international platforms, each with realistic goals and motivated humans. But there is still so much more to be done while keeping up with the ongoing maintenance!

I am trustful that our growing level of awareness will define the stewardship we will play in addressing current ecological issues with the required urgency.

Acknowledgments

A book is never a one-person act of creation.

Neither is caring for our planet. We are all in this together. Acknowledgements go, in no specific order, to:

- Elephants, Flamingos, Rhinos, Giraffes, Koalas, Meerkats, Blue Whales, Ladybugs, Kingfishers, Lobsters, Frogs, Bees, White Leopards, Sea Turtles
- Renaud
- Amy at Studio Friend
- Adam at Good Books Developers
- Santiago Mantas
- Clementine
- Sir David Attenborough (Sir, this book is dedicated to you)
- The Art of Everyone
- Monika at Natural Integrity
- Artichoke Print Workshop
- Supportive Friends and Family
- Planet Earth
- The Universe

About Florina

Florina Falce published her first book, *Everything Else*, in 2019. The book was intended to give a voice to her inquisitive self, someone who asked big life questions and found small and powerful answers. Creativity was one of the answers, and it resulted in the creation *The Art of Everyone*, an online publication presented in collaboration with Publishing Genius Press.

As we can have as many voices as there are causes to support and ideas to explore in this world, Florina's next creative assignment was this chapbook, which is meant as a love message to the wild animals, complemented by Jane Bristowe's beautiful art work.

As much for children as it is for parents and anyone else who loves art and nature, *Dear Elephant* is intended to bring a brief moment of awareness about some of the sufferings the wild animal kingdom faces—but mostly it encourages connection with other life forms on this planet. In order to establish that connection we try to get to know the other being, better understand their circumstances, their nature, their role, their fears, their habits and habitats.

Because when we truly connect with other beings we feel less inclined to dominate or destroy, and more inclined to cultivate love.

Florina spends most of her time in London, where she lives with her husband and daughter.

About Jane

Jane Bristowe, Artist Printmaker, was shortlisted for Wildlife Artist of the Year for her Rhino linocut and her Meerkats linocut was exhibited at the Royal Academy Summer Exhibition. Her style has established Bristowe as a leading exponent of animal images.

Her innovative linocuts display her inventive artistic imagination in capturing the simple appearances and character of a stunning array of animals—and have placed Bristowe among the best of this genre currently working today.

Bristowe's sassy linocut style makes her work immediately recognisable and appealing. Her bold single colour work creates an instant rapport with her subject matter and conveys not only the likeness of each character Bristowe has drawn but it's individual personality as well.

In recent years collaboration and conservation has been key to Bristowe's work in light of the destruction of large swathes of the animal world.

Printed in Great Britain
by Amazon